Novels for Stu[
Volume 14

GW00684640

Staff

Editor: Jennifer Smith.

Contributing Editors: Anne Marie Hacht, Michael L, LaBlanc, Ira Mark Milne, Daniel Toronto, Carol Ullmann.

Managing Editor, Content: Dwayne D. Hayes.

Managing Editor, Product: David Galens.

Publisher, Literature Product: Mark Scott.

Literature Content Capture: Joyce Nakamura, *Managing Editor*. Sara Constantakis, *Editor*.

Research: Victoria B. Cariappa, *Research Manager*. Sarah Genik, Ron Morelli, Tamara Nott, Tracie A. Richardson, *Research Associates*. Nicodemus Ford, *Research Assistant*.

Permissions: Maria L. Franklin, *Permissions Manager*. Shalice Shah-Caldwell, *Permissions*

Associate. Deborah Freitas, *IC Coordinator/Permissions Associate.*

Manufacturing: Mary Beth Trimper, *Manager, Composition and Electronic Prepress.* Evi Seoud, *Assistant Manager, Composition Purchasing and Electronic Prepress.* Stacy Melson, *Buyer.*

Imaging and Multimedia Content Team: Barbara Yarrow, *Manager.* Randy Bassett, *Imaging Supervisor.* Robert Duncan, Dan Newell, Luke Rademacher, *Imaging Specialists.* Pamela A. Reed, *Imaging Coordinator.* Leitha Etheridge-Sims, Mary Grimes, David G. Oblender, *Image Catalogers.* Robyn V. Young, *Project Manager.* Dean Dauphinais, *Senior Image Editor.* Kelly A. Quin, *Image Editor.*

Product Design Team: Pamela A. E. Galbreath, *Senior Art Director.* Michael Logusz, *Graphic Artist.*

agency, institution, publication, service, or individual does not imply endorsement of the editors or publisher. Errors brought to the attention of the publisher and verified to the satisfaction of the publisher will be corrected in future editions.

This publication is a creative work fully protected by all applicable copyright laws, as well as by misappropriation, trade secret, unfair competition, and other applicable laws. The authors and editors of this work have added value to the underlying factual material herein through one or more of the following: unique and original selection, coordination, expression, arrangement, and classification of the information. All rights to this publication will be vigorously defended.

The Pigman

Paul Zindel

1968

Introduction

Paul Zindel's first novel, *The Pigman*, published in
New York in 1968 by Harper & Row, is a story of
two dispossessed young people who find a
surrogate parent in Angelo Pignati, an Italian man
who has never had children and whose wife is dead.
He shares his humor and joy in life with them, and
in his presence, they are allowed to be carefree and
childlike in a way that they can't be with their own
families.

The novel is considered by many critics to be

the "first truly [young adult] book," according to Teri Lesesne in an interview with Zindel in *Teacher Librarian*. When Zindel wrote the book, he realized that few books depicted teenagers dealing with real problems in the modern world. He also talked to many teenagers who said they hated to read or had been branded as troublemakers, and he targeted his story to them. Zindel's honesty and humor "broke new ground, and prepared the soil" for many excellent young adult books to come, according to Lesesne.

In an interview with *Scholastic* students, Zindel said that he was inspired to write the book while he was house-sitting in a fifty-room "castle" on Staten Island. A teenage boy trespassed on the grounds, and when Zindel went out to yell at him, he found out that the boy was actually a very interesting person. The character of John Conlan in *The Pigman* was modeled on this young man. The character of Lorraine was modeled on a student in one of the chemistry classes Zindel taught. He told the interviewer, "I thought, what a wonderful adventure it would be to team those two life models for me into a story in which they met an eccentric, old mentor figure."

Author Biography

Paul Zindel was born on May 15, 1936, in Staten Island, New York, and grew up on Staten Island with his mother and sister. His father, a police officer, abandoned the family when Zindel was very young, and Zindel rarely saw him. His mother struggled to make ends meet, and because of their poverty, the family moved often. Zindel felt like a misfit because he had no father and because the family moved so much, but later realized that this feeling of being different from others had fueled his imagination. He wrote his first play in high school, and enjoyed the praise he got from other students for his morbid sense of humor.

He attended Wagner College on Staten Island, where he studied chemistry, but also took a creative writing course with famed playwright Edward Albee, who encouraged Zindel to write more plays. He wrote his second original play during his last year of college.

After college, Zindel worked briefly as a technical writer for Allied Chemical, but he hated the job. After six months, he quit and became a high-school chemistry and physics teacher. While teaching, he continued to write plays; his first staged play was *The Effect of Gamma Rays on Man-in-the-Moon Marigolds*, loosely based on his own life. The play won several awards, including Best American Play and the Pulitzer Prize for Drama; it was produced on Broadway; and it was made into a film and a television drama.

Charlotte Zolotow, an editor for the publisher Harper & Row, was impressed by the play and asked Zindel if he had any novels in mind. She encouraged him to write *The Pigman*, his first novel, which was published in 1968. The novel was selected as one of the Notable Children's Books of 1940–1970 by the American Library Association and was named one of their Best of the Best Books for Young Adults in 1975. It was also one of the Child Study Association of America's Children's Books of the Year in 1968, and was given the Boston Globe-Horn Book Award for Text in 1969. The book was inspired by two teenagers Zindel met, a young man who had many of the adventures that later appeared in the book, and a young woman who was very much like Lorraine, one of the two main characters. The Pigman, an eccentric old Italian man, was based on an Italian grandfather who was a mentor to Zindel when he was young.

In 1969, Zindel quit teaching and became a full-time writer. In a profile published on the *Scholastic* Web site, he said, "I felt I could do more for teenagers by writing for them." He read several young adult books and felt that they had nothing to do with what teenagers were really like, and he resolved to write honestly from the teenagers' point of view. Since then, he has written many acclaimed books for young adults, including *My Darling, My Hamburger, I Never Loved Your Mind, Pardon Me, You're Stepping on My Eyeball!, The Undertaker's*

Gone Bananas, Confessions of a Teenage Baboon, Raptor, Loch, The Doom Stone, Reef of Death, and most recently, *Rats*.

In 1973, Zindel married Bonnie Hildebrand. They have two children, David and Elizabeth.

In the *Scholastic* profile, Zindel wrote, "I like storytelling. We all have an active thing that we do that gives us self-esteem, that makes us proud; it's necessary. I have to tell stories because that's the way the wiring went in."

Told in chapters alternating from Lorraine's and John's point of view, *The Pigman* opens with an "Oath," signed by both John and Lorraine, two high school sophomores, in which they swear to tell only the facts, in this "memorial epic" about their experiences with Angelo Pignati, whom they later refer to as the "Pigman."

Harmless Pranks Accelerate

John, one of two protagonists who act as narrator, explains that he hates school, in fact hates "everything," and tells about his past escapades, in which he set off firecrackers in the school bathroom and organized his whole class to roll damaged apples across the classroom floor when the substitute teacher had her back turned. Intelligent, charming, and bored, he's not a bad kid, but is pent-up and restless, with parents who don't understand him and don't want to try.

Lorraine, the other protagonist and narrator of the book, is similarly alienated from her family, which consists only of her mother. Her father, who left when her mother was pregnant with her, is now dead, and her mother works as a private nurse to try and make ends meet. Like John, Lorraine is very intelligent; she wants to be a writer. A keen observer of people, she is compassionate and sensitive. She and her mother moved into John's neighborhood at the beginning of freshman year, and Lorraine and John, perhaps drawn by their mutual restlessness and alienation, have since become good friends.

Lorraine and John, with two other friends, play more pranks outside of school. They devise a game in which the challenge is to call strangers on the phone and keep them on the line for as long as possible by telling outlandish stories. Picking numbers at random from the phone book, Lorraine eventually calls Angelo Pignati, an old man who lives in their neighborhood. He's only too happy to talk to them, and when Lorraine tells him they're calling from a charity and asking for money, he unwittingly offers to give them ten dollars.

Lorraine thinks the joke has gone too far and wants to end the phone call, but John gets on the line and makes arrangements to pick up the money from Mr. Pignati at his house. John tells her Mr. Pignati is probably lonely and will welcome their company.

They Meet Mr. Pignati

Mr. Pignati is thrilled to see them. His house, though messy, smells warm and inviting, and he offers them wine and food, and invites them to come to the zoo with him. He explains that his wife, who usually goes with him, is out of town. He shows them his collection of porcelain pigs, plays a game with them, and gives them the ten dollars.

The next day, they go to the zoo with him and

visit his "best friend," Bobo, a vicious baboon. Mr. Pignati seems oblivious to the baboon's nasty personality, and he talks lovingly to the animal and feeds him peanuts and other treats.

Lorraine and John continue visiting Mr. Pignati, lying to their families about where they are going. He tells them to make themselves at home and, while exploring his house, they find funeral documents that show that Mr. Pignati's wife, Conchetta, is actually dead, not on vacation. Her clothes are still in her closet, and Mr. Pignati misses her so much that he can't stand to admit she's really gone.

They Experience Joy in Life

Mr. Pignati takes them on a shopping spree for gourmet delicacies, which his wife loved, and buys roller skates for all three of them. Carefree, they eat the food, drink wine, and listen to his jokes. All of this is a sharp contrast to their own homes, which are depressing and humorless. In John's house, everything is so neat and clean that no one can relax, and his father is always lecturing him about responsibility and trying to force him to be someone he's not, urging him to get a job on Wall Street.

In Lorraine's house, her mother hassles her about hanging out with boys, asks her to stay home from school to clean the house, won't let her use the phone, makes derogatory comments about her appearance, and occasionally hits her. John and Lorraine end up going over to Mr. Pignati's house every day after school for wine and conversation, and become the children Mr. Pignati never had. Eventually they confess that they were never affiliated with any charity, and that they like him more than anyone else and want to be honest with him. In response, he tells them what they already know, that his wife is actually dead, not on vacation.

John begins roller-skating in Mr. Pignati's house, and soon Mr. Pignati and Lorraine join in, but the exercise is too much for Mr. Pignati, who has a heart attack. They call an ambulance and, at the hospital, pose as his children so they can get in to visit him. He tells them to make themselves at home at his place while he's in the hospital, and they do, but they begin overstepping boundaries: Lorraine dresses up in some of Conchetta's clothes, John wears some of Mr. Pignati's, and they pretend to be adults. The fancy evening clothes awaken their awareness of each other as sexual beings, and they tease each other and kiss, but this change in their relationship makes both of them uncomfortable, so they stop and put their own clothes back on. However, they can't take back what they've begun to feel for each other.

A Betrayal and Its Consequences

John decides that while Mr. Pignati is gone, it can't hurt to have a few friends over for a quiet party. Neither of them can have friends over at home, so it's tempting. The quiet party grows into a huge, rowdy, loud, and drunken revel, with about forty teenagers. Norton Kelly, a delinquent, steals an electrical apparatus from the house, and other kids, including Lorraine, get dressed in Conchetta's clothes. John goes after Norton for stealing, and in revenge, Norton smashes Mr. Pignati's precious collection of pigs, which belonged to his wife.

In the midst of this chaos, Mr. Pignati comes home and finds his house in a shambles and the people he loved and trusted, John and Lorraine, at the center of the chaos. They feel horrible, apologize, and try to make amends by asking him to go to the zoo with them to see Bobo. However, when they get there, the cage is empty, and a bored attendant tells them Bobo is dead.

The accumulated shocks and losses prove to be too much for Mr. Pignati, and he suffers a second heart attack and dies immediately. The two young people are left with the realization that his death may be their fault, and with an awareness of the sadness of his life and death, and life and human mortality in general. They realize that time is passing, that someday they, too, will die, that they may spend their later years alone and lonely, and they better grow up and get moving. As John says at the end of the book, "Our life would be what we made of it—nothing more, nothing less."

The Bore

See Mr. Conlan

John Conlan

John Conlan is a fifteen-year-old high-school sophomore who lives in Staten Island, New York, and is best friends with Lorraine Jensen, another student. He is good-looking, charming, and highly intelligent, but is bored with school and with life in general, and his humorless, joyless family life doesn't help. His father, known as "The Bore" to John, is a broker on the coffee exchange. The Bore is interested only in money and stocks, and urges John to get a similar job on the exchange as soon as he's able. John says, "I've been over to the Exchange and seen all the screaming and barking the Bore has to do just to earn a few bucks, and if he thought I was going to have any part of that madhouse, he had another thing coming."

John is also dismayed by his father's stressful lifestyle, and comments, "He's almost sixty years old, and I know he's not going to be around much longer. All the guys on the Exchange drop dead of heart attacks." John's father is oblivious to his son's lack of interest in finance, or to his creative talent, and responds with "Don't be a jackass" when John tells him he wants to be an actor. John's mother is an anxious, obsessively clean woman whose perfectionism fills up her whole life. Both of his parents constantly extol the virtues of his older brother, Kenneth, who is eleven years older than John and who works on the Exchange, just like John's father. John's life at home is hedged in by rules: his mother tells him what to eat and drink and cautions him not to make a mess and not to disturb his father, and his father urges him to become a responsible citizen, to get off the phone, cut his hair, and not disturb his mother, among many other things.

In response to their colorless style of living, John makes his own life more colorful. He exaggerates, lies, and invents dramatic pranks to amuse himself and others. He sets off firecrackers in the boys' bathroom, organizes his whole class to roll rotten apples across the classroom floor whenever there's a substitute teacher and, when his father puts a lock on the family phone to prevent John from using it, John fills the lock with glue so that the Bore can't use it either. Then John figures out a way to dial it anyway, so he's the only one who can use it. With Lorraine Jensen and some other friends, he begins a campaign of telephone games, culminating in one game in which the teenagers tell outlandish lies and try to keep a stranger talking for as long as possible.

In addition, John drinks and smokes more than any other boy Lorraine has ever known. His drinking is a habit started by his father, who used to give John beer when he was a boy and then praise him and laugh at him. He knows drinking and smoking are bad for him, but persists because his life is so oppressive that he feels there's no point in living a long life anyway.

Underneath his colorful exterior, John is sensitive and compassionate. Lorraine suspects that this is why he became her friend, because he had compassion for her loneliness. They are allies because both of them are lonely and alienated from their families.

Mr. Conlan

John Conlan's father, whom John calls "the Bore," works on the Coffee Exchange on Wall Street, and his life is totally subsumed in his job. His son says, "If he sells more than two hundred lots in a day, he's in a good mood. Anything less than that, and there's trouble." He is bothered by his son's apparent flightiness and his creative and disobedient streak, and notices only his superficial qualities, such as his long hair and his constant wisecracking humor. He doesn't see his son as he is —creative, intelligent, and talented—but wants to force him into a mold and remake him as a carbon copy of himself. He tells John, "At your age I was working hard, not floundering around in a fool's dream world."

Mr. Conlan was a compulsive drinker for most of John's childhood, and encouraged John to drink, too. When John was a toddler and young boy, his father would give him sips of beer at parties, and everyone present would laugh as he downed them. "A chip off the old block," Mr. Conlan said proudly, making it seem like drinking was a sign of manhood. Mr. Conlan was eventually diagnosed with cirrhosis of the liver and had to quit drinking, but by that time his son was used to alcohol and kept drinking. Of course, ironically, Mr. Conlan still doesn't think of him as a man.

Mrs. Conlan

John Conlan's mother, whom John calls "hyper" and "the old lady," is terrified of conflict, dust, dirt, and disorder of any kind, and spends her time dashing around cleaning, polishing silverware, monitoring her husband's and John's moods, and trying to smooth over the clashes between them. Her perfectionism makes it impossible for her to really listen to or converse with her son or her husband; the family's house, which she keeps as neat as a museum, is impossible to relax in because everything is either covered with plastic or is off-limits.

Hyper

See Mrs. Conlan

Lorraine Jensen

Lorraine Jensen is a fifteen-year-old high-school sophomore who lives in the same Staten

Island neighborhood as John Conlan, her best friend. She is intelligent and thoughtful, is interested in psychology, and wants to be a writer. She moved into John's neighborhood at the beginning of freshman year, and the first few weeks were torture for her. She was depressed and isolated because she didn't know anyone, and she was shy and insecure about her looks. She met John on the bus, when he sat next to her one day and started laughing. At first she was offended, thinking he was laughing at her, but then she began laughing, too, and from that day on, they were friends.

Lorraine calls herself "paranoid," because she's worried that others don't think much of her, but this is clearly a response to the way her mother has always treated her. Her mother has always told her how ugly and clumsy she is, and at the same time, repeatedly warns her about the evil intentions of men and boys and tells her never to be alone with them. Perhaps because of her sensitivity, she is very compassionate toward others, particularly people she perceives as underdogs. Her compassion is unusual among teenagers; for example, she writes movingly of a poor teacher who keeps her elderly and ill mother in the living room of her apartment, and about Mr. Pignati, whose wife has died.

Mrs. Jensen

Lorraine's mother, a private-duty nurse, has raised Lorraine by herself. Lorraine's father left when she was pregnant with Lorraine, after cheating on her. He has since died, and the burden of single parenthood has fallen heavily on Mrs. Jensen. Since then, she has been fixated on how terrible her husband was, and how terrible men are, in general. This bitterness has soured her life, as well as her relationship with her daughter.

She's constantly making negative comments about Lorraine's hair, clothes, weight, and behavior, and Lorraine says, "If I made a list of every comment she's made about me, you'd think I was a monstrosity." Mrs. Jensen is very pretty when she lets her hair down and relaxes, but this seldom happens; she carries a weight of sadness and depression with her, and has a cynical attitude toward the terminally ill patients she takes care of. Because she believes she's not being paid enough, she steals things from them to even up the score: light bulbs, cleaning supplies, food. She has no shame about this, and no shame about the fact that when a patient dies, she refers their family to a funeral home that pays her ten dollars whenever she sends them some business. Money, or the lack of it, is constantly on her mind, and overtakes all other values. Instead of encouraging Lorraine to stay in school and get good grades so she can do well in the future, she asks her to stay home and clean the kitchen—with cleanser stolen from a dying patient. "I think you could take a year off from that school and not miss anything," she says, and Lorraine knows that if she told her mother she wants to be a writer, she'd never hear the end of it.

Norton Kelly

Norton Kelly is a student in Lorraine's and John's class, and John describes him as "a social outcast." He was once caught stealing a bag of marshmallows from a supermarket, and ever since then he's been taunted as "The Marshmallow Kid." He has a mean streak, and when he finds out that John and Lorraine have access to Mr. Pignati's apartment, he asks if Pignati has anything worth stealing. His mean streak started in childhood, when he got caught playing with dolls and all the other kids harassed him about it; after that, he went berserk and "turned tough guy all the way," according to John. From then on, he spent his time picking fights, throwing stones, beating up people, and calling all the other boys sissies. Since then, Norton has become a thief, shoplifting and stealing whenever he can. John says, "Then he got even worse, until now his eyes even drift out of focus when you're talking to him. He's the kind of guy who could grow up to be a killer." At a party in The Pigman's house, Norton steals an oscilloscope and breaks the old man's precious pig figurines, which were one of the few reminders of The Pig-man's dead wife Mr. Pignati had left.

The Old Lady

See Mrs. Conlan

The Pigman

See Angelo Pignati

Angelo Pignati

Angelo Pignati, called "The Pigman" by Lorraine and John, is an Italian man in his late fifties. Trusting and good-natured, he offers to give them ten dollars when they call him up and pretend to be with a charity. The first impression they have of him is that he has a "jolly voice," and when Lorraine, who's making the call, starts laughing out of nervousness, he asks what the joke is, so he can laugh at it, too, and then tells her a joke. He tells her his wife, who's in California visiting his sister, loves his jokes, and then he talks on and on, telling joke after joke. Lorraine realizes that he's "terribly nice … but also lonely."

He is both, and he's also poor; his house is rundown and messy, but when they go over to his house, he meets them with a huge smile. Unlike their families, he's filled with a sense of enjoyment of life despite his problems. He plays games with them, invites them to go to the zoo with him, and shows them his wife's collection of pig figurines, which she began when she married him and changed her name to Pignati.

Mr. Pignati's wife is actually dead, and he has few friends, but he goes to the zoo frequently to visit and feed his "best friend," Bobo, a vicious baboon. The zookeeper dislikes Bobo because he's mean-tempered, but Mr. Pignati is so pure of heart that he can see no evil in anyone or anything, and believes Bobo is filled with all the love and kindness he himself feels.

Unlike the joyless families of John and Lorraine, Mr. Pignati knows how to have fun. Instead of filling their conversation with rules, he offers them wine and other delicacies, takes them on a shopping spree for luxury foods, buys them (and himself) roller skates, and the three of them roller skate throughout his house and have impromptu parties whenever the teenagers visit. With him, they can be children in a way that they never could with their parents.

Conchetta Pignati

Conchetta is Angelo's wife, and at the time of the story, she has been dead for several months. She is present in the story, however, through his memories of good times with her and through the pleasant habits he has continued: cherishing his collection of pigs, shopping for gourmet foods, and visiting the zoo. She was a sweet woman who always laughed at his jokes, and her possessions are still in his house.

Relationships with Parents

Both John and Lorraine have poor relationships with their parents, who regard them as disturbing burdens. Lorraine's father is dead, and her mother makes ends meet by working as a private-duty nurse. Mrs. Jensen's ethics and values are questionable: she steals from her patients, gets kickbacks from the undertakers she refers patients' families to, and urges Lorraine to stay home from school so she can clean the apartment. Lorraine feels sorry for her mother, but it's evident that these issues make her deeply uncomfortable. In addition, Mrs. Jensen projects her fears about men into Lorraine's life, hassling her about any contact she might have with boys, how dangerous boys are, and how men only have one thing in mind. These comments are not conducive to helping Lorraine develop a healthy understanding of adult relationships, so she must rely on her own instincts and on her friendship with John and Mr. Pignati to learn about what men are really like.

John's parents regard him as a disturbance that must be controlled, molded, and shaped into a carbon copy of his father, who leads an emotionally restricted and stressful life as a trader on the Coffee Exchange. They view John's energy, desire for fun, and dramatic talent as liabilities rather than gifts.

Their household, like Mrs. Jensen's, is cold and not nurturing; he is constantly compared to his brother, who according to his parents is an ideal son. This coldness and comparison to an ideal he does not want to emulate foster a sense of alienation and rebellion in John, and this alienation and rebellion in turn prevent him from focusing his energy on anything productive.

Consequences

John and Lorraine, like many teenagers, have little sense of the consequences of their actions, and they learn that their acts have consequences only when it's too late to change anything. At first, they tell themselves that they're just having fun—just going over to Mr. Pignati's, just having a little party, just having a good time. The party, of course, gets way out of hand, and the shock eventually leads to Mr. Pignati's death. They both realize that they were involved to some degree in his death, but differ in the amount of responsibility they're willing to take. John doesn't take full responsibility, but Lorraine does, as she says, "We murdered him."

Near the end of the book, however, John says after Mr. Pignati's death, "We had trespassed too—been where we didn't belong, and we were being punished for it. Mr. Pignati had paid with his life. But when he died something in us had died as well." This is not an explicit claiming of responsibility on John's part, but the reader senses that he isn't going to be throwing any more wild parties. As he says,

"There was no one else to blame anymore.... And there was no place to hide." He has realized that his actions will have consequences, sometimes dire, and he will have to answer for them.

Topics for Further Study

- In the book, Mr. Pignati has a major effect on John and Lorraine. Write about an older person who affected your life in a way you'll never forget, and how they influenced you.

- John does not believe that he and Lorraine are totally responsible for Mr. Pignati's death, but Lorraine does. In your opinion, who is right, and why? If John and Lorraine were put on trial for killing him, what would the verdict be? Why?

- Mr. Pignati has lived a very lonely

life since his wife died; he has no real friends until John and Lorraine come into his life by accident. Do some research to find out how most elderly people live. Is Mr. Pignati's isolation unusual, or typical? How does the American treatment of elderly people differ from the way they are treated in other cultures?

- John and Lorraine's parents don't talk to their children, and they often act as though the children are a disturbing burden. Do you think this is typical, or are most parents effective? Write a short essay about what it takes to be a good parent.

- John smokes and drinks, even though his father became ill from alcohol and he knows both habits are bad for his health. Why would he do these things if he knows they may eventually kill him?

Life and Death

The book is filled with images and questions about life and death. Lorraine's father is dead, and her mother comes home daily with gripes and callous words about her dying patients; for example, of one old man, she says, "I wish this one would hurry up and die." She compares different funeral homes, considering which one will offer her a bigger kickback if she refers clients to them. Her callous attitude toward death is balanced by Lorraine's extreme sensitivity to suffering and death. This sensitivity leads her to feel sympathy for Mr. Pignati, who still suffers from the loss of his wife.

In Mr. Pignati's house, John and Lorraine find documents from Conchetta Pignati's funeral and read them with mingled sadness, horror, and fascination. Zindel reproduces some of these documents verbatim in the book, perhaps because most young people would be as interested in this glimpse of the adult world as Lorraine and John are.

Before Mr. Pignati's death, John has been unaffected by death, although several of his relatives have died. He didn't feel close to them, so the body in the casket looked "just like a doll." He says, "It gave me a feeling like being in Beekman's toy department to tell the truth—everything elaborately displayed." Because he was emotionally unconnected to the deceased, he is remote from the situation, viewing it in a superficial, childish manner. However, he is aware that he does this to avoid dealing with his fear of death: "Anything to get away from what was really happening." All this changes, of course, when Mr. Pignati dies and John is personally touched by the loss. He can't hide anymore, can't disconnect like he has in the past.

In addition, John, who feels dispossessed and alienated by his family, has picked up a number of self-destructive habits, such as smoking and drinking, and at one point Lorraine tells him, "You must want to die." He doesn't really have an answer for this, and near the end of the book he says, "Maybe I would rather be dead than to turn into the kind of grown-up people I knew." However, he realizes that this is not the answer either, and says with a new resolve, "Our life would be what we made of it—nothing more, nothing less."

Point of View

Zindel's *The Pigman* is told from the point of view of its two main protagonists, who claim they are typing the story in the school library as the librarian, who thinks they're working on a book report, looks on. Chapters written by Lorraine alternate with chapters written by John; both tell the story in the breezy but honest and irreverent style of adolescents, focusing on action more than on internal feelings, motivation, or consequences, although these do sometimes appear in the narrative.

By using two narrators with slightly different points of view to relate the story, Zindel gives the reader a more complete picture of the narrative. In many cases, John or Lorraine will go back and comment on something the other one has written, giving their own version of the events.

Extracts from "Real Life"

An interesting feature of the book is the occasional insertion of handwritten elements, such as John and Lorraine's signatures on an "Oath" to tell the truth about the incidents described in the book; some graffiti John writes on a desk; and some pencil-and-paper games Mr. Pignati plays with them. The book also has a page from a booklet on funeral planning, a bill for a funeral, and a piece torn out from an advice column. These elements add realism and immediacy to the story, making it even more believable.

Foreshadowing

In keeping with teenagers' tendency toward drama, Lorraine frequently notes "omens" that, in hindsight, she believes should have warned her that something terrible was going to happen. This foreshadowing is not subtle; for example, she describes her visit to the zoo with John and Mr. Pignati, where a woman selling peanuts is rude to her. "That was the first omen," she writes. "I should have left right on the spot." The second omen occurs when a peacock, seeing that she has a bag of peanuts in her hand, chases her, and a third one occurs in the Mammal Building, where she sees a child who is watching the people who've come to watch the vampire bats. "He made me feel as though I was a bat in a cage and he was on the outside looking at me. It all made me very nervous," she writes. In another omen, when she and John go downtown with Mr. Pignati, she sees a mentally ill woman who keeps repeating "Death is coming. God told me death is coming." In another scene, Lorraine dreams that she finds a long black coffin in Mr. Pignati's house. Although these "omens" might seem like ordinary occurrences to many readers, or in some cases, logical consequences of her fears about Mr. Pignati's survival after his heart attack,

Lorraine's willingness to read a more global and deeper meaning into them is typical of the teenage point of view, and also warns readers that some as-yet-unidentified disaster will occur in the course of the book.

Dialogue

Zindel's style is heavily dependent on dialogue, perhaps because of his background as a playwright. The dialogue is skillfully written and extremely natural; Zindel has a true ear for the way teenagers, and adults, talk to each other. In addition, because the book is "written" by John and Lorraine in alternating chapters, even the narrative or descriptive parts of the book have a unique teenage flavor. The book begins:

> Now, I don't like school, which you might say is one of the factors that got us involved with this old guy we nicknamed the Pigman. Actually, I hate school, but then again most of the time I hate everything.

Artfully, Zindel kept the book from becoming dated by using language that sounds like slang, but has a minimum of slang terms, which can quickly become stale for readers. In chapter 3, John explains this principle, which Zindel seems to have adopted: "I really hate it when a teacher has to show she isn't behind the times by using some expression which sounds so up-to-date you know for sure she's behind the times." Instead of using slang current at the time the book was written, Zindel has his teenage characters use language that suggests slang, with words such as "dimwit," "nutty," and "crazy," and phrases such as "five-finger discount," "putrid brand of beer," and "these two amoebae" (referring to two delinquent boys). John calls his mom "The Hyper" or "The Old Lady" and he calls his dad "The Bore."

Instead of using curse words, he tells the reader that he will use the symbol "@#$%" for "a mild curse—like the kind you hear in the movies"—and "3@#$%" for a "revolting curse," "the raunchiest curse you can think of." This use of symbols has two benefits for Zindel and the reader: readers can insert whatever curses they are familiar with, thus keeping the book current, and because Zindel doesn't spell out the offending words, adult readers will have no objection to his use of them in a young adult novel.

Historical Context

The Pigman was written in the late 1960s, a time when American society was in an uproar. Protests against the Vietnam War, the growth of the Civil Rights and feminist movements, and a vigorous celebration of teenagers and young adults as the new, free generation were set against those who wanted to preserve the status quo and traditional values. Zindel's book was groundbreaking in its truthful depiction of teenagers who were not respectful to their teachers, whose parents had failed them, and who engaged in actions adults would disapprove of—such as minor vandalism, drinking alcohol, and smoking. Before the publication of The Pigman, few books for young adults were so open and truthful; instead, books tended to portray an ideal world in which adults wished teens would live.

Although Lorraine and John love their parents, they are open in their criticism of how their parents have failed them, a common complaint of the younger generation during the 1960s and early 1970s. "Never trust anyone over 35" was a commonly heard phrase among rebellious youths, who believed there was more to life than wearing a suit and making a living. As John tells his father, "I just don't want to wear a suit every day and carry an attaché case and ride a subway. I want to be *me*. Not a phony in the crowd." This celebration of creativity and individualism, which when taken to an extreme led the '60s generation to be labeled "The Me Generation," is typical of young people of that time. John's father, uncomprehending and scornful, insists that John's ambition to be an actor is "a fool's dream world," a comment typical of the older generation of that time. Interestingly, John's brother Kenneth, who is eleven years older, has remained on the older generation's side of the divide: he has accepted his father's values and works on Wall Street.

Another feature typical of the younger generation of that time is a pervasive distrust of anyone in authority, such as teachers, police officers, and parents. Both John and Lorraine have vast areas of their lives their parents know nothing about. Although Lorraine is less scornful of her mother than John is of his parents, she realizes that her mother is too wounded to help her or to understand what she's involved in, and she lies to her mother about what she's up to. John is more bitterly disappointed by his parents, and shows it by blatant disobedience and backtalk. When the police show up after Mr. Pignati's heart attack, John calls them "snotty" and "dumb," and both he and Lorraine lie to the police about being Mr. Pignati's children. He also says, after they leave, "They were probably anxious to get along on the rounds of the local bars and collect their graft for the week." Lorraine, who is not as cynical, is angered by this comment and tells John she hopes he needs the police someday but can't find an officer to help him.

Compare & Contrast

- **1960s:** Teen smoking, drinking, and drug use become prevalent in the 1960s, when knowledge of the ill effects of drugs is still not widespread, and when a widespread sense of experimentation and rebellion is part of popular culture.

  Today: Teen smoking and drinking have increased since the 1960s, and every day, about 3,000 young people begin smoking. Nearly 1,000 of that number (1 in 3) will eventually die as a result of smoking-related disease. Use of cigarettes, alcohol, and drugs is more common among teens who do not feel emotionally connected to their parents.

- **1960s:** Not everyone can afford a telephone, and instead of using touch-tones, phones use a rotary dial system. Phone numbers have two letters and five numbers, like "Sa7-7295," the number for the hospital Mr. Pignati is in. The two letters are an abbreviation of the name of the "exchange," usually a neighborhood. Faxes, personal computers, and the Internet are unknown.

  Today: Phone companies have dropped the letter-and-number system in favor of all-numeric phone numbers, and the old rotary phones are considered obsolete; many telephone services cannot be accessed unless the caller has a touch-tone phone. The number of people needing phone numbers has continued to increase, so that every year, phone companies must create new area codes. In addition, cellular phones, fax machines, pagers, and the Internet allow people to be constantly connected to each other, even if they are on the other side of the world.

- **1960s:** In the 1960s, AIDS is unknown, and people don't worry about many of the consequences of sexual activity. Rates of teen pregnancy, divorce, and single-parent families are higher than those of earlier decades, and people regard these issues as shameful.

  Today: AIDS has forced many people to reassess their sexual activity and to take precautions against this and other diseases. However, divorce rates continue to increase, and teen pregnancies and single-parent families are now common. Attitudes toward divorce, teen pregnancy, and single parenting have changed, so that many people now regard these issues as painful, but without the sense of shame and blame that was still prevalent in the

1960s.

- **1960s–1970s:** The Vietnam War rages throughout the 1960s and early 1970s, sparking widespread anti-war protests in the United States. Throughout the war, in which 3 million Americans serve, 58,000 Americans die, 1,000 are declared missing, and 150,000 are wounded.

  Today: The United States has been involved in several smaller wars since the 1960s, most notably the Gulf War in the Middle East, but none have incited such widespread commentary and rebellion as the Vietnam War has. However, the hijacking of three planes on September 11, 2001, and the attacks on the World Trade Center Towers in New York and on the Pentagon in Washington D.C. are the largest terrorist attacks to date.

It's interesting that Zindel chose not to mention any of the political and social events, such as widespread protests, riots, and rallies, as well as the Vietnam War, which were taking place at the time that he wrote the book. Perhaps he did this in order to avoid making the book seem dated; more likely, he chose to do this because it's true to life. Many teenagers are unaware of political and social events, or only peripherally affected. For many teens, life at school, interactions with parents, and activities with friends take center stage in their lives.

Critical Overview

The *Pigman* is widely acknowledged as a turning point in young adult literature. According to Jack Davis Forman in *Presenting Paul Zindel*, Zindel's "commitment to write realistically about the concerns of teenagers" set his books apart from "the previous genre of teen fiction calcified in the gender and age stereotypes of the 1950s." Forman quoted Kenneth Donelson and Alleen Nilssen, whose survey, *Literature for Today's Young Adults*, noted that *The Pigman* "established a new type of adolescent fiction in which teenagers dealing with interpersonal or societal problems were depicted with candor and seriousness."

As Forman noted, previous books had portrayed teenagers as adults wished they were, or thought they should be, and were "pedestrian, predictable, and formulaic." Zindel was one of the first writers to show teenagers from a teenage point of view, unfiltered by adult notions of right, wrong, or what their behavior should be. According to Forman, a reviewer in *Horn Book* called *The Pigman* "a now book," and commented that few books were "as cruelly truthful about the human condition." Forman also noted that a *New York Times* reviewer wrote that the book had "the right combination of the preposterous and the sensible," but commented that Zindel's overt explanation of the book's "moral" was patronizing to readers. Forman also quoted *Publishers Weekly* reviewer

Lavinia Russ, who remarked on her excitement at discovering such a skilled new writer by saying she felt "like the watcher of the skies when a new planet swam into its ken."

In *English Journal*, Loretta Clarke praised the book, except for the ending; like the *New York Times* reviewer, she felt that the last three lines were weak:

Baboons.

Baboons.

They build their own cages, we could almost hear the Pigman whisper, as he took his children with him.

"These three lines intrude upon the story," Clarke wrote, but commented that otherwise, Zindel "has reflected through his adolescent writers an adolescent view of life."

In *Teacher Librarian*, Teri Lesesne wrote that the book was "one of those touchstone books that set apart novels for adolescents," that it "set the standard for writers to follow," and that it "is considered by many to be the first truly YA [young adult] book."

The book was listed as one of the Child Study Association of America's Children's Books of the Year for 1968, and won the Boston Globe-Horn Book Award in 1969. It was also listed as one of the American Library Association's Best Young Adult Books in 1975.

What Do I Read Next?

- *The Effect of Gamma Rays on Man-in-the-Moon Marigolds*, published in 1964, was Zindel's first play, and won the Pulitzer Prize for Drama in 1971. The play stars Tillie, a brilliant girl who lives with her epileptic sister and her overbearing mother; through her success in science, Tillie is able to break free from her stifling family.

- *I Never Loved Your Mind* (1970), Zindel's third novel, stars high school dropout Dewey Daniels and his true love, fellow dropout Yvette Goethals.

- In Zindel's *My Darling, My Hamburger* (1969), a high school girl discovers she is pregnant, but her abusive parents are no help, so she decides to visit an illegal abortionist.

- Zindel's *Pardon Me, You're Stepping on My Eyeball!* (1976) tells the story of two misfits who head out for adventure.

- In Zindel's *The Pigman's Legacy* (1980), a sequel to *The Pigman*, John and Lorraine visit the Pigman's empty house and find an old man who's hiding from the tax authorities. They see him as their chance to make up for how they treated the Pigman, and launch into new adventures.

- S. E. Hinton's *The Outsiders* tells the story of a high school "greaser," or delinquent, who hates the rich, popular kids—until his friend murders one of them, and he must come to terms with his beliefs about people and life.

Sources

Clarke, Loretta, "The Pigman: A Novel of Adolescence," in *English Journal*, Vol. 61, No. 8, November 1972.

Forman, Jack Davis, *Presenting Paul Zindel*, Twayne Publishers, 1988, pp. 12-17, 57-59.

Lesesne, Teri, "Humor, Bathos, and Fear: An Interview with Paul Zindel," in *Teacher Librarian*, Vol. 27, No. 2, December 1999, p. 60.

Zindel, Paul, "Paul Zindel: Interview Transcript," *Scholastic*, http://teacher.scholastic.com (June 14, 2001).

——————————, "Paul Zindel's Booklist," *Scholastic*, http://teacher.scholastic.com (June 14, 2001).

For Further Reading

National Council of Teachers of English, *Speaking for Ourselves: Autobiographical Sketches by Notable Authors of Books for Young Adults*, National Council of Teachers of English, 1990.

> This compendium of autobiographies features Zindel and many other writers for young adults, who discuss their lives and works.

Raymond, Gerard, "The Effects of Staten Island on a Pulitzer Prize-Winning Playwright," in *Theater Week*, Vol. 2, No. 37, April 24, 1989, p. 16-21.

> The article discusses Zindel's difficult upbringing and its ramifications for his writing.

Rees, David, *The Marble in the Water: Essays on Contemporary Writers of Fiction for Children and Young Adults*, Horn Book, Inc., 1980.

> This collection of essays provides critical insight on the works of contemporary novelists who write for children and young adults.

Zindel, Paul, *The Pigman and Me*, HarperCollins, 1992.

> Zindel's autobiography discusses his painful childhood, his career as a writer, and the inspiration for his

work.